Make a Bottle Garden

Claire Llewellyn

Contents

What is a bottle garden?   2
What you need   4
Choose your bottle   6
Get your bottle ready   8
Choose your plants   10
Make your tools   12
Plant your garden   14
Glossary and Index   16

What is a bottle garden?

A bottle garden is just what it says – it is a tiny garden inside a large bottle or jar. This kind of garden looks good and is very easy to look after. You only need to water it every two months.

Making a bottle garden is very easy. This book tells you how. You could make a garden just for yourself, but it would also make a lovely present.

What you need

Here is everything you will need
to make a bottle garden.

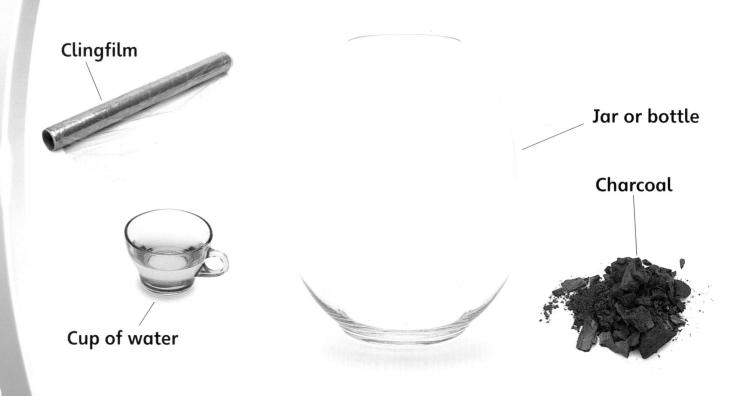

Clingfilm

Jar or bottle

Charcoal

Cup of water

Small houseplants

Potting compost

Canes (about 30 cm long)

Gravel

Sticky tape

Fork

Scissors

Cotton reel

Spoon

5

Choose your bottle

What kind of bottle or jar will you need for your garden? It must be big and tall, and have a wide neck so that you can get your hand inside. A big sweet jar would work well. So would an old fish bowl or tank.

Your jar can be made of glass or plastic, but the walls of the jar must be clear so that light can get in. All plants need light to grow, so wash and dry your jar very well.

Now you are ready to begin!

Get your bottle ready

Get your bottle ready for your plants by putting in layers of **gravel, charcoal** and **compost.**

compost (about 10 cm)

charcoal (about 2 cm)

gravel (about 3 cm)

1 Put a layer of gravel in the bottom of the bottle.
The gravel helps to drain your plants.
If the compost gets too wet,
water runs down into the gravel.

2 Put a thin layer of charcoal on top of the gravel. Charcoal keeps the compost from smelling bad.

3 Put a thick layer of compost on top of the charcoal. Compost gives the plants food.

Choose your plants

You will need about four or five tiny **houseplants** for your garden. Choose plants that will look good next to one another – some tall and some short, some light green and some dark green, and plants with different kinds of leaves. Do not use flowering plants, or cacti, or plants that grow very fast. Here are some plants that will grow well in a bottle garden.

Make your tools

You need tools to plant your garden, but most tools are too big to go inside a bottle. You need to make your own mini tools instead. Turn to page 5 to see what you will need.

1 Use sticky tape to fix a **cane** to the handle of a spoon. This makes a mini spade.

2 Use sticky tape
to fix a cane
to the handle
of a fork.
This makes
a mini garden fork.

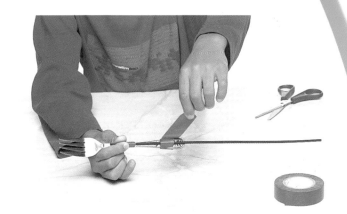

3 Fix a **cotton reel**
onto the end of a
cane with sticky tape.
This tool is good
for patting down
the compost.

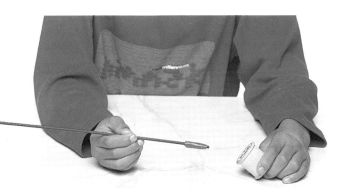

Plant your garden

Now it is time to plant your garden!

1. Use the spoon and fork to dig a hole in the compost and put in a plant.

2. Use the cotton reel to pat down the compost around the plant.

3. When you have put in all the plants, water them with a cup of water.

4. After a few days, put a lid or clingfilm on your jar. This keeps all the water in. Add a spoonful of water every two months.

5 Now put your garden in a
light place – but not in
the sun – and sit back
and watch it grow.

Glossary

cane	small straight stick
charcoal	black lumps of burnt wood
compost	fine soil that is good for houseplants
cotton reel	spool for holding thread
gravel	small pebbles
houseplants	plants that will grow indoors

Index

bottle	2, 4, 6
charcoal	4, 8, 9
compost	5, 8, 9, 14
gravel	5, 8, 9
plants	5, 10, 14